Parenting Your Rising Star

For Success, Joy and Fulfillment

Parenting Your Rising Star

For Success, Joy and Fulfillment

By
Ted W. Sieja, MD
Pediatrics

Cathedral City, California, USA
2025

Parenting Your Rising Star, for Success, Joy, and Fulfillment

© 2025 Ted W. Sieja, MD, Pediatrics

All rights reserved. No part of this publication may be reproduced, distributed, or transmitted in any form or by any means, including photocopying, recording, or other electronic or mechanical methods, without the prior written permission of the publisher, except as permitted by U.S. copyright law. For permission requests, contact the publisher.

This book contains brief quotations from historical figures and public personalities.

Quotations from authors and government officials whose works are in the public domain are reproduced freely.

Selected quotations from modern figures are used sparingly and are reproduced for purposes of commentary, education, and inspiration. Their inclusion is consistent with the principles of fair use under United States copyright law (17 U.S.C. §107).

Every quotation is cited and attributed to its source. Some entries are noted as "Attributed to…" where authorship or exact phrasing is uncertain.

No endorsement of this work by the quoted individuals, their families, or their estates is implied.

All other content in this work is © Ted W. Sieja, MD, Pediatrics, 2025. All rights reserved.

One half of the author's proceeds from sales of the books will be donated directly to:
• Shelters for expectant women and women with children
• Books for families of limited means

First paperback edition October 2025
Book design by AquaZebra.com

Library of Congress Control Number: 2025920611
ISBN: 978-1-954604-20-9

Published by AquaZebra
35070 Maria Road
Cathedral City, CA 92234
aquazebra@gmail.com

Dedication

For Wendy, my mom, and all the new and experienced mothers of the world. Thank you for your selfless love, time, devotion, and just plain hard work. Yours is the most challenging and difficult job in the world. We cannot thank you enough. You are the true unsung heroines of the world.

Acknowledgments

I would like to thank my book publisher, Mark E. Anderson, AquaZebra.com, and my colleague Adam Cox, host of The Hypnotist Podcast, for their support, direction, belief in me, and the book's essential role in parenting today.

Prologue

Any endeavor or journey in life, if not done for human reasons with love and understanding, will be a very empty and lonely one. This is worth thinking about as we live in a time, as Einstein noted (paraphrasing from a 1946 letter), when our technology is rapidly surpassing our humanity.

The quality and fulfillment in life are determined by the thoughts you have, decisions you make, and actions you take. This is the foundation for a successful life.

Our Dream
Using love, science, and technology to raise humanitarians.

I believe it is up to mothers and fathers to save our planet and future generations. Governments have not been successful. Just look around or turn on the news. The wisest karate sensei teaches you that you win every fight you prevent or avoid. Pediatricians know the best medicine is preventing illness. The only way to change our future is to be proactive. Mothers are the best sources to teach our children that humanity must once again be valued above materialism. Only then can our children create a better future for the world and generations to come.

Paraphrasing *The Greatest Love* of All sung by Whitney Houston, states the dream: *I see the next generation as the path forward. Guide them with care and allow them to take charge of their journey. Help them recognize the goodness and potential within themselves, and nurture their confidence so challenges feel lighter.*

This parenting book, put into action, is the best way to make our dream come true. Why do you think they call our home Mother Earth?

Paraphrasing Willie Wonka's Mother: *All great achievements begin as dreams — so never let go of yours.* It's in your arms now. It's up to you.

Foreword

Dear Mom and Dad,

After more than thirty years of pediatric practice and wellness coaching, I conclude that what parents truly need most is caring emotional support and the belief that they are *good enough* to raise a happy, healthy child. Of course, they all wanted to be the "perfect parent" and not screw their kids up. (Their words, not mine.)

The basics of parenting, the how-to and what-to-do-when, are covered in many excellent child-rearing books, such as those written by T. Berry Brazelton and Heidi Murkoff. They include all the essentials and are reassuring.

You, like all good parents, want the best for your children: to become happy, fulfilled, and prosperous adults. This book is a guide for how you can do that. If you trust yourself a little and follow the advice with commitment and persistence, you will give your childen the cornerstones to a wonderful life.

The four cornerstones are:
1. Self-love and acceptance
2. Self-belief and confidence
3. Compassion and kindness
4. Gratitude

With these cornerstones, love and support, your children will have the foundation to build a dream life for themselves.

It is a sad fact, but the two core fears of adults today are: "Am I good enough?" And, "Am I worthy and deserving of love?" Well, you are! Everyone is, and if you don't believe it yet, you will. With consistent work and following the book's instructions exactly as written, your newborn will show you by growing into a most amazing person. You must read the book over and over. **Newborns learn by repetition and observation.**

Use your imagination and put your heart into it. Every successful woman or man will tell you they have achieved success by practicing, step by step, for years. And, Of course, they all owe it to their mothers, fathers, and other caregivers.

Finally, believe in yourself. Over the years, I have seen the most insecure parents learn and grow into excellent parents, simply by following the book's instructions day after day. Enjoy your newborn and have fun.

You are a family now.

Ted W. Sieja, MD
Pediatrics

"It's not the destination, it's the journey."
— Attributed to Ralph Waldo Emerson, often linked to *Self-Reliance* (1841), though exact phrasing is uncertain.

"Take the first step in faith. You don't have to see the whole staircase, just take the first step."
— Dr. Martin Luther King, Jr., speech, 1962.

Introduction

Dear Mommy and Daddy,

…If only I could talk…

The first thing I would tell you is "Thank you for having me." Second thing: "Miracles really do happen, and you are holding one in your arms right now, and I am looking at one. Please don't ever forget that."

Now, on to business. If you read this little book to me every night, it won't take very long, but it will make the best bonding experience between us, leading to a life of great value, fulfillment, love, and fun times. It will guide you to what I really need and not what the rest of the world says I need and can't live without. They are businessmen who tell you fulfillment comes from what you have: a great job, an expensive home, a trendy car, money, and status. But a successful life with joy and fulfillment comes from who you are. So please read our book, as Dr Sieja says. Simple things repeated over and over produce awesome results. It's how you will teach me to walk, learn my ABCs, ride a bike, and make you crazy when I learn to drive.

After a few months, when the words have settled in and taken root, it's time to begin putting them into action. Take one thought or idea daily and turn it into play during the day. Just use your imagination! It is a scientific fact that I live in an imaginary world until I'm six years old. Please do it until then. This action step makes it a part of who we are now and the adult I become. ***It creates my identity, for life.*** Remember, great thoughts without action are like prayers without faith. So, with repetition, we grow and create the family every parent wants and deserves.

Ted W. Sieja, MD, Pediatrics

Just remember, there is no perfect way or perfect parents. I'll do best if you follow the book's instructions. Please, pretty please, keep an open mind, follow your instincts, and trust what your hearts tell you. Most of all, believe and have faith in yourself, as I already do. That's it! It's simple and it works!

Gratefully,
Me, aka Cutie Pie, Peanut, Pumpkin, Sweat Pea, Muffin

P.S. Actually, as science now demonstrates, it will work if you start reading it to me even before I'm born.

Contract

Mommy and Daddy, before you sign this contract, close your eyes for one minute and imagine how much more amazing your life would be if your parents had this book to guide them and to ease their anxiety.

Well, you do have this book, so be confident in your ability to raise me. You are the world's greatest parents. Just follow the instructions, and I promise to embody the positive feelings, beliefs and have the best habits ever. That's my best for you. (I promise, no fingers crossed.)

Thank you in advance for giving me your best as well.
Love,
An awesome adult in the making, just ask Aristotle.

"Excellence is not an act, but a habit. We are what we repeatedly do."
— Will Durant, paraphrasing Aristotle,
The Story of Philosophy (1926).

Ted W. Sieja, MD, Pediatrics

We, _____ and _____, parents of _____ will read this book every night before sleep and each morning beginning on page 1 to the end of the book.

We understand our gentle touch, kind tone of voice (not ga-ga, goo-goo stuff), and our smiling faces will create a strong and loving bond between the 3 of us.

We believe the heartfelt wisdom in this book will instill the necessary cornerstones for a fulfilled, happy, and successful life for you and our family.

We freely sign this contract and will diligently follow through on our commitment. We only want the best for you.

Parent's Signatures   _____
                      _____

    Before you start reading this book twice a day, turn to the four blank pages at the end. Use these pages to write down life lessons and advice that you want to share with your child such as things that are important to you like your beliefs, values, and hopes for them.

    A long time ago, a famous philosopher named Aristotle said, "Give me a child until he is 7 and I will show you the man." He meant that children are open to learning and growing, and what they learn early stays with them forever. In a way, this book was inspired by him, one of the most famous thinkers ever.

    Let's get started…

Remember, above all, I will always love you and need you.

Ted W. Sieja, MD, Pediatrics

Let Go of the Need for Perfection

- You don't have to know everything to be my mom. Just know I love and believe in you, and everything will fall in place.
- Believe in yourself and have faith in your abilities like I do.
- Trust in your instincts. It usually works out for the best.
- Even if you don't always get it right, it's really no big deal. We all make mistakes. Life and Nature are never perfect, but they are miraculous and beautiful.

Household chores and errands can wait. They really are not that important.

- What is truly important is the time we spend together.
- It is okay to cry. I do it all the time.
- And it really does get easier, Mom and Dad.

Keep in Mind
- You will not always know what I want, and that's no big deal.
- Neither do I.
- What do I want?
- What do I need?

What I want and need is YOU!

Repeat after me:
- "I can't control everything. Life just happens."

Now repeat again:
- "I can't control everything. Life just happens."

Here is the secret:
- No one else really does control everything. They just act like they do.
- Don't you feel better?

Ted W. Sieja, MD, Pediatrics

Be gentle, kind, and forgive yourself. You deserve it!
- Never feel guilty about taking care of yourself. If you are not healthy, how will I ever learn how to be that way?
- Show me that one of the most important values to possess in life is good health. With it, you can do anything.
- When we eat well, exercise and play, and take naps, we grow up to be healthy, happy, and successful.
- Naps are important for both of us.
- Remember that you cannot do everything and that you will need help. We all do from time to time.
- You must make some free time for yourself. With all that you do, you deserve a break.
- Appreciate how wonderful you really are. I do every day.
- If you have a partner, let him or her help with bathing me and changing my diaper.
- Be as grateful for me as I am for you.

You are Doing an Amazing Job

- Judge your success as my mother by the way I smile at you. It's the only opinion that really matters.

- Don't worry about the future. Life only comes one day at a time for both of us.

- Always remember, every one of my smiles is a thank you. Life is beautiful.

Ted W. Sieja, MD, Pediatrics

BE FIRM, KIND, AND CONSISTENT WITH ME.

BE PROUD OF ME.

Ted W. Sieja, MD, Pediatrics

Always follow through on what you say.

Help me become the Best Person I can be.

- Remember the saying, "Prepare the child for the Path, not the path for the child."
- Make a list of your values and be an example of them.
- I learn more from your actions than what you say.
- The values you teach me early will be my moral compass for life.
- Measure me by the values that you have instilled in me and not by my height and weight.
- Your influence on me is beyond measure. Be firm and gentle. I don't break, but I do bounce!
- Show me how to live a rich, full life.
- Please hold me to your high standards and accept nothing less than my best.
- Always be proud of who I am becoming. What I accomplish is not as important.
- I do things at my own pace, so there's no need to compare me to other kids.

- Always measure me by the size of my heart and kindness, not my accomplishments.
- What you tell me, I take literally and believe. Be generous with praise.
- Give me family traditions as a strong foundation, not as limitations.
- Keep my toys simple so I can be interactive with my imagination and creativity.
- Help me to improve on just one thing every day.
- Help instill a positive and encouraging voice inside my head.
- Encourage me to spend time by myself.
- Always focus on making things a little better, not bigger and busier.
- Please never criticize who I am, just my "bad behavior". Then help me to correct it.
- My life is more secure when you are tough-minded and tender-hearted.

"Imagination is more important than knowledge. For knowledge is limited, whereas imagination embraces the entire world."
 — Albert Einstein, Quoted in *The Saturday Evening Post* (1929).

Ted W. Sieja, MD, Pediatrics

Never lose sight of our dreams. Because if you do, all you will see is piles of dirty diapers.

"Focus more on your desire than on your doubt, and the dream will take care of itself."

— Attributed to Mark Twain, though not present in *A Connecticut Yankee* in King Arthur's Court (1889).

- If you pursue your dreams and follow your heart, I will learn to follow Mine.
- Never give up on your dreams, never let me lose sight of mine.
- Talk to me about your hopes and dreams, and they will help shape mine.
- Continuously reinforce the idea that anything is possible.

"A winner is a dreamer who never gives up."

— Nelson Mandela, c. 1990.

- Instill in me a courageous spirit to prepare me for life.
- Help me build a foundation of strength and courage so I can reach for the stars.
- I know I can always lean on you but encourage me to stand on my own.
- Give me the hope and faith I need to face the many challenges of life.
- No need to worry when I fall or cry. Just encourage me to stand on my own and to learn to trust myself. I already trust you.

"Do not judge me by my success, judge me by how many times I fell down and got back up again."
 — Attributed to Nelson Mandela, paraphrase from early 1990s speeches.

Ted W. Sieja, MD, Pediatrics

No Matter where we are or what is happening, I am always at home in your arms.

"All that I am, or ever hope to be, I owe to my angel mother."
— Abraham Lincoln, letter c. 1850.

Bonding: Walk, Talk, Read, Sing

- Take me for a walk every day to share the wonder and magic of nature with me.
- Most worthwhile things in life are difficult. Like raising me, for instance. Always focus on the fun in it.
- We need at least one hour every day in the fun and silly zone. Playing recharges your batteries.
- Remember, you grow old and tired because you quit playing. Not the other way around.
- Please read to me every night before I go to sleep.
- When you are holding me, talk to me. If you talk to me a lot, I will get in the habit of listening to you. That is sure to have a great payoff later when I am in my teens.
- Singing is even better. Your voice is like magic to me. Like listening to a famous concerto by Beethoven or Mozart.
- "Presents" are great. But I'd prefer your "presence."
- Material possessions don't hold a candle to your time and attention.
- I want you to cherish every moment that we have together, the way I do.
- So, let's create lots of memories now. We will both cherish and need them later.

Repeat after me: "I can't control everything. Life just happens."

Now again: "I can't control everything. Life just happens."

Here is the secret.

- No one else really does control everything. They just act like they do.
- Ring a bell? I can't say this enough… Just get over it!
- Show me how to focus on what I can control. That way, I can do my best when I go into our uncontrollable world.
- I can control my thoughts.
- I can control my feelings and emotions.
- I can control my behavior.
- With that and the self-belief, courage, and strength you taught me to have, I will feel good enough and okay. That's all we need anyway.

"You only have control over yourself."
— Oprah Winfrey, *Master Class*, 2011.

"You cannot always control what goes on outside. But you can always control what goes on inside."
— Wayne Dyer, *Your Erroneous Zones* (1976).

Ted W. Sieja, MD, Pediatrics

A BAD DAY CAN STILL BE SAVED WITH A HUG AND A KISS FOR NO REASON.

LOVE IS THE REASON!

Love is all you Need

- My love for you is unconditional. Just as yours is for me.
- Be yourself, I love you just as you are.
- You can never love me too much, but you can overprotect me.
- Whenever you hug me, you are giving and receiving love. It feels great, doesn't it?
- When I succeed, give me a hug. When I fail, give me a hug and then show me how to improve.
- Never underestimate the power your love has to shape me.

Ted W. Sieja, MD, Pediatrics

It's moms, not models, who are the most beautiful women in the world.

"My mother was the most beautiful woman I ever saw. All I am I owe to my mother."
— Attributed to George Washington
(source uncertain; long-standing oral attribution).

If you ever feel discouraged or that nobody cares, just look into my eyes, and you will see just how important your love is to me.

- You are the best mom I will ever have, and that is plenty for me.
- I just know you are always behind me, 100%.
- Remember the old proverb: "God couldn't be everywhere, so he created mothers."
- Also, remember that Hollywood and the media will be promoting their "values" 24/7.
- Just stick to your own values, and we will be just fine.
- I'm growing!
- I'm learning!
- And getting stronger every day!

"Education is the most powerful weapon which you can use to change the world."
— Nelson Mandela, Madison Park High School speech, Boston, 1990.

- I learn mostly by what I see and hear.
- Sometimes it's not what you do for me, but what you have taught me to do for myself.
- Boundaries, discipline, and schedules make me feel safe and secure. (Ouch, that one hurt to say)
- Discipline and teaching me to do the right thing are acts of Love.
- Last but not least… Don't worry about teaching me everything. There are lots of things I'll need to learn on my own.
- I would however, love it if you could teach me some of these things.

Teach Me

- To help make the world a better place for everyone.
- Mankind is our biggest family, and we are all brothers and sisters.
- To be kind and to forgive everyone, especially the less fortunate and animals.
- How to make the best situation out of a bad situation.
- To strive for excellence, not perfection.
- To see my limitations and how to grow beyond them.
- To be a good winner and loser.
- To apply knowledge learned with action.
- To become the hero of my story.

"Education is not the learning of facts, but the training of the mind to think."
— Attributed to Albert Einstein, 1920s lectures (exact wording varies).

Teach Me
- Nothing is as important as it first seems.
- To never underestimate my abilities.
- That pain and disappointment are a part of life.
- To never compromise my integrity.
- To see joy and happiness in every moment, and how to create it on rainy days.

Teach Me

- That the core of self-esteem and self-respect comes from working towards something.
- Not to fear failure.
- That you can learn more from your failures than your successes.
- That in forgiveness, you can let go of things.
- To never be afraid to try new things.
- That you don't really know what you like until you try it.

Teach Me
- To always keep an open mind and open heart.
- To never lose my faith.
- Not to judge others based on their appearance.
- The value of compassion and gratitude.
- To think big and enjoy the small pleasures in life.

"Children are the world's most valuable resource and its best hope for the future."
— John F. Kennedy, Statement for UN Children's Fund (1963).

Ted W. Sieja, MD, Pediatrics

Teach Me

- That "Please and Thank You" are not just words, but an expression of kindness and gratitude.
- That humanity is more important than technology.
- That happiness and real success are founded upon the friends and family we love and cherish.
- That life is not about avoiding problems but facing and overcoming them.
- That happiness is not lost out there. It is inside of us; we just need to look inside.
- That the only way to reach my dreams is to work for them.

P.S.

You can always read the book or parts of it to me anytime. It's especially helpful on days you've forgotten that you are the most important, needed, and loved mom and dad in the whole world. And the best parents I will ever have!

By the way, this is not the end, but the beginning…

Ted W. Sieja, MD, Pediatrics

Please write in important life lessons to guide your child with your personal beliefs, values, and dreams.

Parenting Your Rising Star

Ted W. Sieja, MD, Pediatrics

Author's Note

Parenting Your Rising Star was born from my own vulnerability, my hopes and dreams for humanity, and my knowledge in both general and pediatric care. This book is meant to guide and inspire parents and children to build strong foundations of purpose, joy, and fulfillment for their families. From that foundation, children can go on to create the lives of their dreams. I believe that living with purpose, joy, and fulfillment is the truest measure of success.

Doctor Ted & Two Socks

I want to honor all parents for their devotion and the unconditional love they so generously give. To the families who were my patients and my teachers, it was an honor to be welcomed into the most important and meaningful journey of your parenting life.

In closing, thank you for the greatest gift imaginable: the privilege of living out my passion and purpose every day. I have done my very best, and I hope your rising stars will take us even higher. In the end, we make it together—or we don't make it at all.

To be useful is to serve a purpose by acting in a way that makes a positive difference in the world and helps others, which contributes to a sense of meaning, happiness, and well-being for the individual. Ultimately, a life of usefulness is about being connected to and serving others, creating a positive impact beyond oneself.

Sincerely,
Dr. Ted

www.ingramcontent.com/pod-product-compliance
Lightning Source LLC
LaVergne TN
LVHW010319070426
835512LV00028B/3495